PROMISES

I Make When I'm

Baptized

at 8

Baptism Activity Book

written by Katie Edna Steed

CFI • An imprint of Cedar Fort, Inc.
Springville, Utah

To my children: Lucy, David, and Vivian.
Thanks for letting me teach you
about Jesus and thank you for teaching
me much more than you will ever realize.

Text © 2020 Katie Edna Steed
Front cover illustration © 2020 Corey Egbert
All rights reserved.

ISBN 13: 978-1-4621-3601-8

Published by CFI, an imprint of Cedar Fort, Inc.
2373 W. 700 S., Springville, UT 84663
Distributed by Cedar Fort, Inc., www.cedarfort.com

Cover and interior layout and design by Shawnda T. Craig
Cover design © 2020 Cedar Fort, Inc.

Printed in the United States of America

10 9 8 7 6 5 4 3 2 1

Printed on acid-free paper

Contents

Introduction 1

My Baptismal Covenant 2

What Are My Baptismal Covenants? 3

Ordinances 7

To Be Called His People 12

Willing to Bear One Another's Burdens That They May Be Light 15

Willing to Mourn with Those That Mourn and Comfort Those That Stand in Need of Comfort 17

Stand as a Witness of God at All Times and in All Things and in All Places That Ye May Be In... 20

Be Baptized as a Witness before Him That Ye Have Entered into a Covenant with Him. 23

That Ye Will Serve Him and Keep His Commandments............................. 27

That Ye May Be Redeemed of God, and Be Numbered with Those of the First Resurrection... 32

That Ye May Have Eternal Life.............. 35

That He May Pour Out His Spirit More Abundantly upon You........................... 38

What Does It Mean to Have a Testimony of God and Jesus Christ? 40

God Is Our Heavenly Father.................. 44

Jesus Christ Is the Son of God 48

What Does It Mean That the Gospel of Jesus Christ Has Been Restored through the Prophet Joseph Smith? 52

Why Did the Gospel of Jesus Christ Need to Be Restored?..................................... 56

Who Is Joseph Smith and How Did He Restore the Gospel of Jesus Christ?...... 58

The Book of Mormon Is Another Testament of Jesus Christ..................... 64

What Does It Mean to Be Confirmed and Receive the Gift of the Holy Ghost? 67

Who Is the Holy Ghost?......................... 70

What Does It Mean to Receive the Gift of the Holy Ghost?......................... 75

What Is Tithing and What Does It Mean to Pay Tithing?...................................... 78

What Is the Word of Wisdom and What Does It Mean to Follow the Word of Wisdom?... 81

What Is the Sabbath Day? 84

What Is the Law of Chastity? 90

What Is Repentance?............................. 92

Do You Believe That the Church President Is a Prophet of God? 96

Taking the Sacrament Each Week Helps Us Remember Our Baptismal Covenants and Stay on the Covenant Path........... 101

Answer Key.. 104

About the Author 106

Introduction

What an exciting time this is! You are preparing to be baptized. President Russell M. Nelson said, "Each day is a day of decision, and our decisions determine our destiny" ("Decisions for Eternity," *Ensign*, November 2013). In deciding to be baptized, you are choosing a life to be close to God. Being close to God will bring you more peace and joy.

This book was designed to help you prepare for your baptism and the covenants you will make. The first part of this book will help you better understand what we read about in Mosiah. You will learn all about your baptismal covenants; things like what it means to comfort those that stand in need of comfort and to mourn with those that mourn. You will also learn the difference between a covenant and an ordinance.

There can be a lot of questions when it comes to getting baptized. The next section was created to help you answer these questions. Learning about things like keeping the Sabbath day holy and paying a full tithe can help you be better prepared to stand as a witness of Christ.

A Primary song we love to sing says, "I like to look for rainbows whenever there is rain and ponder on the beauty of an earth made clean again. I want my life to be as clean as earth right after rain. I want to be the best I can. And live with God again" ("When I Am Baptized," *Hymns*, no. 103). I hope this book will help you as you prepare to be the best you can be.

My Baptismal Covenant

Mosiah 18:8–13

8 And it came to pass that he said unto them: Behold, here are the waters of Mormon (for thus were they called) and now, as ye are desirous to come into the fold of God, and to be called his people, and are willing to bear one another's burdens, that they may be light;

9 Yea, and are willing to mourn with those that mourn; yea, and comfort those that stand in need of comfort, and to stand as witnesses of God at all times and in all things, and in all places that ye may be in, even until death, that ye may be redeemed of God, and be numbered with those of the first resurrection, that ye may have eternal life—

10 Now I say unto you, if this be the desire of your hearts, what have you against being baptized in the name of the Lord, as a witness before him that ye have entered into a covenant with him, that ye will serve him and keep his commandments, that he may pour out his Spirit more abundantly upon you?

11 And now when the people had heard these words, they clapped their hands for joy, and exclaimed: This is the desire of our hearts.

12 And now it came to pass that Alma took Helam, he being one of the first, and went and stood forth in the water, and cried, saying: O Lord, pour out thy Spirit upon thy servant, that he may do this work with holiness of heart.

13 And when he had said these words, the Spirit of the Lord was upon him, and he said: Helam, I baptize thee, having authority from the Almighty God, as a testimony that ye have entered into a covenant to serve him until you are dead as to the mortal body; and may the Spirit of the Lord be poured out upon you; and may he grant unto you eternal life, through the redemption of Christ, whom he has prepared from the foundation of the world.

What Are My Baptismal Covenants?

A covenant is a way that God shows His great love for us. Covenants give us power and blessings and help us return to our Heavenly Parents.

A covenant is often referred to as a two-way promise we make with God. Have you ever promised someone you would do something? Perhaps your Mom has said to you something like, "Once you clean up all of your toys you can go outside and play." When you do this, you promise to clean up your toys, and your Mom's part of the promise is to let you play outside.

When we prepare for baptism, we prepare to make covenants with God. We promise to do things such as help others, be kind, and choose the right. God promises us that we can live with Him forever if we keep these covenants.

Some of the things we covenant to do when we are baptized include being called His people, bearing one another's burdens, mourning with those that mourn, comforting those that stand in need of comfort, and standing as a witness of God. You will learn more about these covenants as you complete the pages in this book.

SCRIPTURES

Mosiah 18:8–10, Jeremiah 31:31–34, Moroni 10:33,
Doctrine and Covenants 97:8, Doctrine and Covenants 98:13–15

3

Some of Our Covenants With God

Directions: Figure out the answers for the crossword puzzle below by filling in the missing words in the sentences provided. **Hint:** you just might find the same sentences somewhere on the previous page to help you.

Down:

1. Bearing one another's _____.

3. _____ with those that mourn.

5. Mourning with _____ that mourn.

6. _____ one another's burdens.

8. Comforting those that stand in _____ of comfort.

Across:

2. Being _____ His people.

4. _____ those that stand in need of comfort.

7. Standing as a witness of _____.

9. Being called His _____.

10. Standing as a _____ of God.

A Covenant is a two-way Promise

Directions: Think of something you might promise someone and what they might promise you. Write down what you will promise on the top blank line, and what someone else will promise you on the line at the bottom of the page. Work together to reach your common goal in the center.

I Promise _____

I Promise that I will Be kind _____

Directions: Take a piece of twine or rope. With a partner, each of you hold a different end of the rope. Place a cloth over the middle of the rope. To find the answer, read the questions below and do what they are asking. Write your answers in the boxes below the questions.

> **What happens when each of you does your part to hold your end of the rope tight?**

> **What happens to the cloth when someone lets go of their end of the rope?**

> **Why is it important that each person hold tight to their commitments and promises?**

Ordinances

A covenant is a promise and an ordinance is a sacred act. A covenant is always paired with an ordinance. This means that every time you make a covenant (or promise) with God, there is some sort of ordinance or action done that goes with the covenant.

When you are baptized, you covenant to do things like help others, be kind, and choose the right. The ordinance (or act) performed with these covenants is when you physically go into the baptismal font and a prayer is said before you are completely covered in the water.

At church we take the bread and water. This is called the sacrament. The ordinance (or act) is when we take the bread and water. The covenants of the sacrament include things like taking the name of Christ upon us and always remembering God.

Directions: Add other people and items that you see in church during the sacrament to the scene below and then color the image.

─ SCRIPTURES ─

Exodus 18:20, Doctrine & Covenants 59:9,
Doctrine and Covenants 124:39

Third Article of Faith

We believe that through the Atonement of Christ,
all mankind may be saved, by obedience
to the laws and ordinances of the Gospel.

Directions: Find all the words from the above article of faith in the word search below. As you find each word, be sure to cross it off the list.

```
R X G O W Z F H Q E V D H I R E U N U N E Z T C K H P P W J
H I S A R V A O C D L X Z V J Q P H Y P X H V H L S U D I M
Y Z U C B L S M H Z G B K A D D Y R H P X L W D N L O T K Z
A E A Y M D P A T O N E M E N T T H F Y Q O C K F F F X K B
N P F S Z R C H R I S T C F X Q B F L W F H H I Q D A P A V
S D Y L D E S N W H Y C X M V D F D M J J M B N U T D S B M
M Y Y A R Z B J L N D M S U O V A R B K F D R M C R H M J G
T R D W B J F Z Y Z G M Y P T F B W P U O C X R Q V U A R D
W C N S I A M C E C Y D C F J P R C D L N A B H I I L O T E
T L O R Q P J A G D I J P H U P D W S C I S Y U H A T U L Y
O V K F Y M Z K Y H K H K C Q B E S W D A I O V S A V E D Q
A Y H O P A M O K W S U W Q F S E B D G O R L E K D M B F V
L G D E S U O U I D W L Z F S K X X L J I B U K S M D H B M
L L E R L W S Y X D E W R S L Q H U M I L E O C D C S C F Q
U D P R W M T N B N B C I A L G K T Z K L O B E D I E N C E
O Y R G R L V X E L I S P V J Y A H V R H R H J S C H L Q B
C D B Q T E Y D L H O B K K M R S V J Z Q E O K U G P W S T
S C Z A H K M V I V S V Y B Y Z Y X V W H C Y F Q C O G V R
L Z U L R H M K E Y C J W T H E X X H R N S L Z A U K Y O U
H W G W O I I R V M P F P U Z H G O S U S H J R A U D C O N
E S H L U B T J E I L C Q Y H I T S U Y T T R Q Z M M C R A
N X L N G F W H K H N V O C M I O G A F P O W F D X C C D U
Q W X W H J J Z G S K M C L H X P I C P L M O G B J F I I Q
I M N D Q Q Z Q F D D A R Y J K A J H F U M Y J R S I S N B
J A T Q O G O S P E L P T O S V Y P U Z I E Z Y C M Z E A T
A O L V V E A J S Q O Q Q N G D U K Y H Z F V T B E G G N O
V H N N T Y Z W A O D D P A V U P F H J A R H H P A W G C A
Q G H G N K J J V O C T T G N W U A B U E D P E R V T E E B
M J V P T X P Q S O N S F H C D M A N K I N D O E V I Z S N
I I L F V S J B R T Z R L B E W W E B O R Q K F H M M W O Z
```

ordinances	believe	saved	and	of	~~by~~
obedience	through	that	may	the	~~of~~
atonement	gospel	laws	the	we	be
mankind	christ	all	the	to	

Fourth Article of Faith

We believe that the first principles and ordinances of the Gospel are: first, Faith in the Lord Jesus Christ; second, Repentance; third, Baptism by immersion for the remission of sins; fourth, Laying on of hands for the gift of the Holy Ghost.

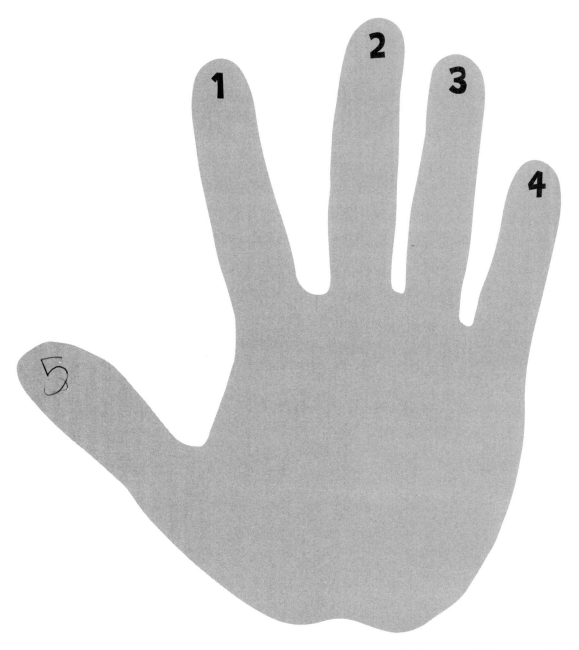

Directions: On each finger, list a principle or ordinance of the gospel that you find in the fourth article of faith.

Fifth Article of Faith

We believe that a man must be called of God, by prophecy, and by the laying on of hands by those who are in authority, to preach the Gospel and administer in the ordinances thereof.

Directions: Add other objects and people that might be in the room when you are set apart for a calling and then color the entire image.

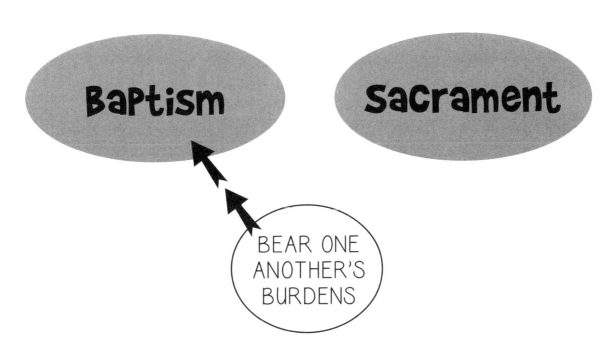

KEEP HIS
COMMANDMENTS

STAND AS A
WITNESS OF GOD

THAT YOU MAY
ALWAYS HAVE
HIS SPIRIT TO BE
WITH YOU.

ALWAYS
REMEMBER HIM

MOURN WITH
THOSE THAT
MOURN

COMFORT THOSE
THAT STAND IN
NEED OF COMFORT

Directions: Match the covenant with the ordinance. The first one is done for you.

To Be Called His People

Have you ever looked closely at a missionary's badge that they wear on their dress or suit for everyone to see? Every missionary badge has two very important pieces of information: **1. The missionary's name**
2. The name of who they represent

Missionaries represent The Church of Jesus Christ of Latter-day Saints. They have made a special commitment to be known wherever they go as God's people—members of The Church of Jesus Christ of Latter-day Saints.

When you are baptized, you also get to show all those around you that you want to be known as one of God's people—a member of His church.

ELDER MISSIONARIES

SISTER MISSIONARIES

SCRIPTURES

Mosiah 18:8

Missionary Badge

Directions: Below is a missionary badge like what you see missionaries wearing all around the world. This missionary badge needs a name filled in. Will you write your name on the badge and color it in? Prepare to make the commitment of baptism and be known as one of God's people.

Question: I can show I want to be called one of God's people by

Answer: _____

_____

_____

THE CHURCH OF
JESUS CHRIST
OF LATTER-DAY SAINTS

Tenth Article of Faith

We believe in the literal gathering of Israel and in the restoration of the Ten Tribes; that Zion (the New Jerusalem) will be built upon the American continent; that Christ will reign personally upon the earth; and, that the earth will be renewed and receive its paradisiacal glory.

Question: Ask an adult to help you understand how choosing to be baptized is part of gathering Israel. Write what you learn.

Answer: _____

_____

_____

Directions: Write the tenth article of faith in the large outline of the number 10.

Willing to Bear one another's Burdens that they may Be light

Part of your baptismal covenant is to help "bear one another's burdens that they may be light." Have you ever tried to carry something that is really heavy? This can be hard to do. A burden is often explained as something that is a heavy load to carry.

Often when we read about things in the scriptures, lessons are being taught in the form of symbols. You see symbols all around you everyday. For example, when you see this, what does it mean?

 **Means:** _____

When we learn about burdens in the scriptures, burdens (or carrying a heavy load) are a symbol for heavy or hard things that someone has to do. For example, I might consider that being asked to clean my room is a burden or a hard thing to do. We can help lift other's burdens when we help them do the hard things they are asked to do.

One day a little girl was at her aunt's house. She noticed that her aunt was working really hard to get her house clean. This little girl decided she could help her aunt by picking up all of the toys and books that had been left out in the room.

She saw that her aunt had some burdens, or some things she was trying to carry or complete. Once she saw this, she stepped in to help. She took the burden her aunt had of trying to clean her house and made it lighter by taking care of some of the things she needed to do. This is an example of "bearing one another's burdens that they may be light."

Directions: Look at the room below. Circle all the things you could do to help relieve someone's burden.

Question: How do you think helping someone with this burden will make them feel?

Answer: _____

_____

Question: How do you think helping them with this burden will make you feel?

Answer: _____

_____

Willing to mourn with those that m
comfort those that stand in need of

Our family had a dog that we loved. His name was Sterling. One day S
sick. There was nothing the vet could do to help him feel better, and our s
We were so sad. One of our neighbor friends came over just after Sterling
still crying. When we told her what had happened, she hugged us and cri

Our sadness became her sadness. Because we were crying, she was also crying. It felt nice to have a friend that loved us enough to feel our sorrow so deeply that our pain was her pain. This sweet story of our friend crying with us in a time we were so sad is an example of what it means to mourn with those that mourn.

Directions: Color by number the activity below to see a picture of our sweet dog.

So Many Emotions

scared, excited, silly, worried, sad, happy, love,
tired, confused, surprised, irritated, mad

Directions: Look at all the different emotions in the faces above. On the lines beneath each face, write which emotion you think best describes what each person is feeling. Use the word list above to help you choose the emotion. It is good to understand the emotions of others so we can better learn how to mourn with those that mourn.

Story Puppets

Directions: Color and cut out the puppets of the little girl and boy above. Using the puppets, act out a story in which one of them gets hurt while riding their bike and the other comes to comfort them.

StanD as a witness of GoD at all times anD in all things anD in all Places that ye may Be in.

When our children were young (ages 3, 5, and 7 years old), our family lived in China for a time. China is a country on the other side of the world from where our family lives now. Many things are the same in China, but many things are different.

We learned very quickly that our blond-haired, blue-eyed children stood out in this country where nearly everyone had black hair and brown eyes. The people of China were so kind and welcoming to us. They would wave and smile at us. If my children were ever playing at a park and got hurt, I could rarely get to them faster than a dear little nainai (Chinese for grandma) could get to them. It was a sweet experience to feel so noticed and loved.

We went to church each Sunday when we lived in China. The process to get to church was quite involved. We would wake up early enough to get dressed in our Sunday best and pack our bag for a trip that would take almost six hours to complete.

First we would walk to our shuttle stop in our neighborhood. Then we would board the shuttle and take it to the bus station. At the bus station, we would catch our bus into the city. Sometimes the bus was so full that we would have to put our children on our laps so everyone would fit. The bus ride into the city took about 45 minutes. Once we were in the city, the bus would drop us off at a stop where we had to walk another 10 minutes to get to church (and this was back when church was 3 hours long).

We did this every week for 16 weeks in order to go to and from church. Some days it was raining, and other days it was sunny. On one of our very last Sundays in China, we met a sweet lady on the bus. She spoke English very well. We had never met this woman before. It was interesting to learn about her and her eight-year-old son.

She explained that they took the bus every Sunday so her son could take piano lessons in the city. After she told us about her son, she looked at us and said, "You ride this bus into the city every Sunday too." Since we had never met this woman, I thought she was asking if we rode the bus every Sunday.

I started to explain that we did ride the bus every Sunday, but she stopped me. She said, "No. I know you ride the bus every Sunday. I see you and your family get on this bus. You are always dressed so nice, and your girls' hair looks so pretty. I think you must be going some place very special."

I was a bit surprised to learn that this woman I had never noticed had noticed our family every Sunday. Before I could say something in return, she looked at me and said, "I think you must go to church. I think it is very good that you do this."

By this point, we had arrived at our stop, and it was time to go our separate ways. As I continued on to church that day, the thought occurred to me how much we could be a witness of God. Even by just doing the simple things like putting on church clothes, doing our hair a little nicer, and carrying scriptures. All of these things helped us to stand as a witness. She could see that we loved God and He was important to us. This woman noticed this witness every single week.

Directions: Think about a time that you have had an opportunity to stand as a witness. In the space above, draw a picture or write down how you were able to stand as a witness.

Be Baptized as a Witness Before Him that ye have entered into a Covenant With Him.

When Jesus Christ asked John the Baptist to baptize Him, John was confused. John knew that Jesus was perfect. John felt that Jesus should be baptizing him. Jesus reminded John that even He, Jesus Christ, needed to be baptized as part of doing all that God wanted Him to do on this earth. When Jesus was baptized, He was being a witness that He wanted to enter into a covenant with God.

One day my daughter came home and told me, "There was a bald eagle at my school today!" "A bald eagle? Are you sure?" I questioned her.

"Yes, there was a real bald eagle!" she replied.

"Are you sure it was a bald eagle?" I continued to question. "It probably was a big bird, but bald eagles are pretty rare."

"Mom, I know it was a bald eagle!" she continued to say.

Just then her older sister walked in and exclaimed, "Mom, this man who takes care of injured birds came to our school today, and he brought a real bald eagle with him to show to our whole school at an assembly. It was so cool!"

Although I was hesitant when one child told me a bald eagle had been at her school, I really started to believe when the second child also told me this story. Each of my children were a witness that day of something they knew to be true. In this case, they were witnesses that a bald eagle had come to their school.

23

Be Baptized as a Witness

Heavenly Father uses witnesses a lot when He wants to make sure sacred things are done correctly. Each baptism is very important to Him. It matters that each baptism is done right.

Two witnesses are used at every baptism to help make sure it is done the correct way. These witnesses will stand close to the font where they can watch and listen to make sure everything that needs to happen at the baptism is done in the right way.

If the witnesses notice anything that is not quite right, like a toe popping up when the person is under the water, they can let the person doing the baptism know, and he can try again. It is not a big deal if anything needs to be done again. The thing to focus on is that your baptism is important to Heavenly Father. He cares, and He wants it to be done just right.

Directions: The image above shows a girl being baptized, but where are the witnesses? Add the witnesses into the image by drawing them in the background then color the entire image.

Preparing for Your Baptism

You are starting to fulfill the covenant of being baptized as a witness of Him by preparing to be baptized.

Directions: Use these pages to help you plan for your special day.

Full Name: _____

When will your baptism be? _____

Where will your baptism be? _____

Who would you like to be at your baptism? _____

Who will baptize you? _____

Who will be the two witnesses for your baptism? _____

Who will confirm you? _____

What songs would you like sung at your baptism? _____

Who will speak at your baptism? _____

Who will say the prayers at your baptism? _____

Draw or put a picture of yourself here.

You can check with an adult to make sure you have done everything that needs to be done for where you live, but this list should help you get started. Check off each item when it's done.

☐ Have a baptism interview with your bishop.

☐ Obtain permission from your bishop for the person who will be baptizing you.

☐ Invite family members and friends.

☐ Let your Primary leaders know.

☐ Schedule the church building or find out when baptisms are held in your area and make sure someone will have the font ready for you.

Another way you can prepare for your baptism is to make sure you have everything you need for your special day. Below is a checklist you can use to mark off what you should bring with you to your baptism.

☐ Wear white underwear when you are baptized so it will not show when you get wet.

☐ Baptism clothing will be provided for you, but some families have their own special white clothes they want to wear when they are baptized.

☐ Dry underwear

☐ Comb, brush, and other hair accessories

☐ Towel

☐ Plastic bag for wet clothes

☐ Some people like to put things on a table at their baptism, like a picture, flowers, or a sign-in book. You do not have to do this, but it is something to think about.

☐ Make sure whoever is baptizing you has all of these things as well.

That ye will serve Him and keep His Commandments

Heavenly Father loves you so much. He knows what is good for you. He knows what will make you strong. He knows what will help you have the Holy Ghost. He knows how you can return to Him. Heavenly Father also knows what is bad or dangerous for us. Heavenly Father gives us commandments to help us know what to do and to bless us. Commandments help keep us safe.

We can read in the Bible in the book of John that if we love God, we should keep His commandments. Moses first taught us about commandments when God gave him the Ten Commandments written on stone tablets.

Commandments can be thought of as rules from God. These rules are given to us to help keep us and those around us safe. When we keep the commandments, we are also able to show respect for God. God has promised us safety and peace when we choose to keep the commandments.

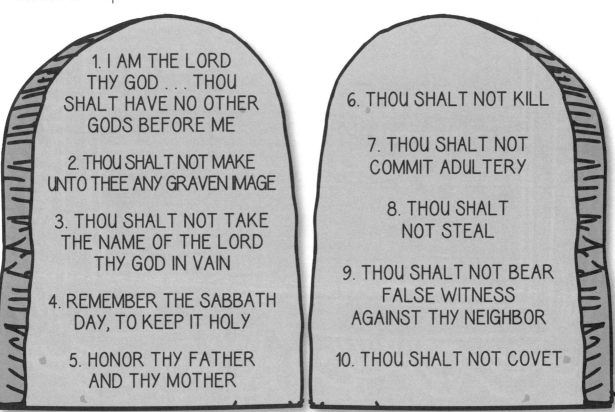

1. I AM THE LORD THY GOD . . . THOU SHALT HAVE NO OTHER GODS BEFORE ME

2. THOU SHALT NOT MAKE UNTO THEE ANY GRAVEN IMAGE

3. THOU SHALT NOT TAKE THE NAME OF THE LORD THY GOD IN VAIN

4. REMEMBER THE SABBATH DAY, TO KEEP IT HOLY

5. HONOR THY FATHER AND THY MOTHER

6. THOU SHALT NOT KILL

7. THOU SHALT NOT COMMIT ADULTERY

8. THOU SHALT NOT STEAL

9. THOU SHALT NOT BEAR FALSE WITNESS AGAINST THY NEIGHBOR

10. THOU SHALT NOT COVET

SCRIPTURES

John 14:15, Exodus 20:1–17

What are the Ten Commandments?

Directions: Practice the ten commandments by writing each commandment inside the numbers below. Use the image on the previous page to find out which commandment is listed first, second, third, and so on.

Twelfth Article of Faith

Directions: Use the code conversion table at the bottom of the page to crack the code and fill in all the letters of the article of faith below.

Question: What does this article of faith have to do with keeping the commandments?

Answer: _____

$\overline{23}\ \overline{5}\quad \overline{2}\ \overline{5}\ \overline{12}\ \overline{9}\ \overline{5}\ \overline{22}\ \overline{5}\quad \overline{9}\ \overline{14}$

$\overline{2}\ \overline{5}\ \overline{9}\ \overline{14}\ \overline{7}\quad \overline{19}\ \overline{21}\ \overline{2}\ \overline{10}\ \overline{5}\ \overline{3}\ \overline{20}\quad \overline{20}\ \overline{15}$

$\overline{11}\ \overline{9}\ \overline{14}\ \overline{7}\ \overline{19}\ ,\quad \overline{16}\ \overline{18}\ \overline{5}\ \overline{19}\ \overline{9}\ \overline{4}\ \overline{5}\ \overline{19}\ \overline{20}\ \overline{19}\ ,$

$\overline{18}\ \overline{21}\ \overline{12}\ \overline{5}\ \overline{18}\ \overline{19}\ ,\quad \overline{1}\ \overline{14}\ \overline{4}$

$\overline{13}\ \overline{1}\ \overline{7}\ \overline{9}\ \overline{19}\ \overline{20}\ \overline{18}\ \overline{1}\ \overline{20}\ \overline{4}\ \overline{19}\ ,$

$\overline{9}\ \overline{14}\quad \overline{15}\ \overline{2}\ \overline{5}\ \overline{25}\ \overline{9}\ \overline{14}\ \overline{7}\ ,$

$\overline{8}\ \overline{15}\ \overline{14}\ \overline{15}\ \overline{18}\ \overline{9}\ \overline{14}\ \overline{7}\ ,\quad \overline{1}\ \overline{14}\ \overline{4}$

$\overline{19}\ \overline{21}\ \overline{19}\ \overline{20}\ \overline{1}\ \overline{9}\ \overline{14}\ \overline{9}\ \overline{14}\ \overline{7}\quad \overline{20}\ \overline{8}\ \overline{5}\quad \overline{12}\ \overline{1}\ \overline{23}\ .$

CODE CONVERSION TABLE

A=1 B=2 C=3 D=4 E=5 F=6 G=7 H=8 I=9 J=10
K=11 L=12 M=13 N=14 O=15 P=16 Q=17 R=18
S=19 T=20 U=21 V=22 W=23 X=24 Y=25 Z=26

The Thirteenth Article of Faith talks about the admonition of Paul.

We can read about the admonition of Paul in Philippians 4:8.

Finally, brethren, whatsoever things are true, whatsoever things are honest, whatsoever things are just, whatsoever things are pure, whatsoever things are lovely, whatsoever things are of good report; if there be any virtue, and if there be any praise, think on these things.

Directions: Find words in the word search below that teach us about the admonition of Paul.

Question: How will following the admonition of Paul help us keep God's commandments?

Answer: _____

_____

```
J  U  S  T  J  Y  S  V  W  A  X  P  X  D  J  G  L  O  E  W
P  V  G  Q  F  Z  M  D  I  Q  Y  H  O  N  E  S  T  V  J  R
H  A  Z  U  M  X  T  U  T  J  U  W  D  L  S  G  P  R  M  L
H  E  O  C  E  Q  A  D  S  F  W  U  O  Q  M  E  H  S  V  O
X  K  A  O  X  W  P  J  X  O  K  D  S  A  G  K  U  F  O  B
X  P  Y  N  I  S  D  W  L  Q  Z  F  B  P  B  Q  Y  D  V  G
W  O  P  Y  N  F  K  E  W  B  Q  L  U  H  T  O  L  N  H  L
T  X  D  E  V  H  Z  L  U  W  A  G  C  H  U  U  B  H  K  I
O  V  O  I  R  V  I  S  N  P  Q  K  T  K  N  E  M  B  M  N
Y  G  C  L  W  A  F  H  D  Z  A  W  Z  K  A  I  M  H  D  V
O  R  S  I  J  M  L  D  T  B  L  V  M  V  I  K  O  F  Q  T
O  A  T  Z  B  P  A  W  W  W  T  A  B  T  A  Q  T  R  U  E
J  P  L  W  V  S  T  U  A  H  V  W  A  P  W  L  I  V  P  V
W  A  Z  L  C  C  D  L  Y  M  D  X  U  U  R  B  V  B  E  I
P  N  M  G  L  X  G  O  O  D  U  Q  H  R  S  O  C  X  X  A
B  R  T  G  V  M  Q  V  V  I  R  T  U  E  P  S  N  S  J  T
E  Q  V  J  O  Y  S  E  L  W  V  D  J  B  X  R  U  X  L  M
A  L  Q  M  P  F  Y  L  M  T  S  W  B  R  W  J  E  L  S  T
H  D  D  M  F  O  P  Y  M  Z  A  Z  Q  R  I  C  Z  A  D  J
I  X  F  O  W  M  B  K  R  O  J  S  C  U  U  O  W  M  X  N
```

Find these words:

true

honest

just

pure

lovely

good

virtue

Thirteenth Article of Faith

Each word strip below is a part of the thirteenth article of faith. The problem is, they are not in the right order.

Directions: Cut the strips out and see if you can put the thirteenth article of faith back together in the right order.

WE HAVE ENDURED MANY THINGS, AND

GOOD REPORT OR PRAISEWORTHY, WE SEEK

DOING GOOD TO ALL MEN; INDEED, WE MAY SAY

AFTER THESE THINGS.

THAT WE FOLLOW THE ADMONITION OF

HOPE TO BE ABLE TO ENDURE ALL THINGS. IF

CHASTE, BENEVOLENT, VIRTUOUS, AND IN

WE BELIEVE IN BEING HONEST, TRUE,

PAUL—WE BELIEVE ALL THINGS, WE HOPE ALL THINGS,

THERE IS ANYTHING VIRTUOUS, LOVELY, OR OF

That ye may Be redeemed of God, and Be numBered with those of the first resurrection

When we die, our bodies and spirits are separated. Resurrection is when after a person has died, their body and spirit are reunited. The wonderful thing about a resurrected body is that it will be perfect and won't get sick or die ever again.

Everyone will be resurrected; however, not everyone will be resurrected at the same time. Those who choose to be baptized and follow God will have the opportunity to come forth in the First Resurrection.

SCRIPTURES

1 Corinthians 15:22, Luke 24:39, Alma 11:41–43,
2 Nephi 9:6, Mosiah 15:19–26

Your Spirit and Your Body

See if you can find a glove. We can think of our bodies as being like a glove. The glove is not really able to do much on its own. It needs something. It needs our hand! Putting a hand inside a glove is like having our spirit in our body. When our body and spirit are together, we are alive.

When you take off the glove, it can be compared to when we die. The spirit and the body are no longer together. Just like the glove cannot move without a hand in it, the body cannot move without a spirit in it.

What happens when you put the glove back on? The glove can move all around again. This is like being resurrected.

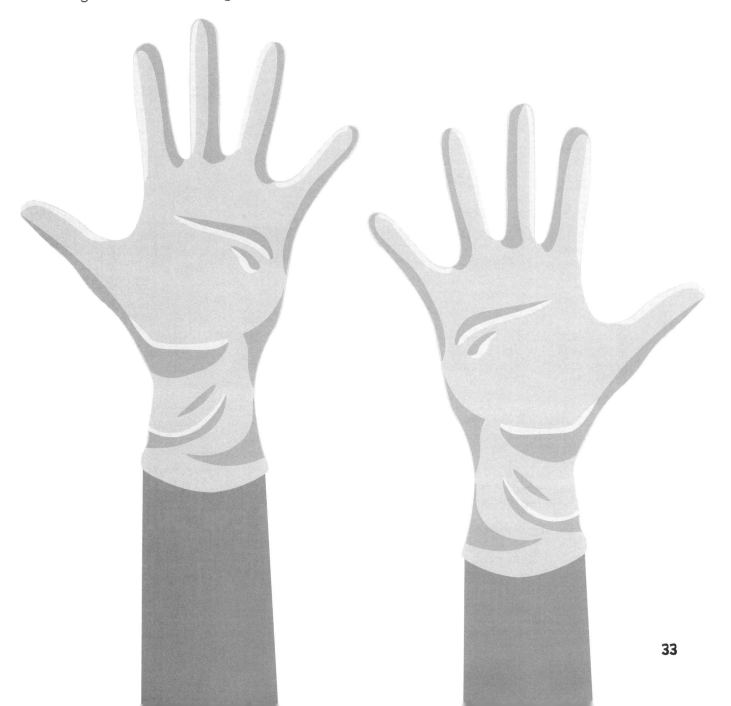

33

Recipe for Empty Tomb Rolls

Our family loves to make empty tomb rolls.

We can think of the marshmallow as Jesus's body that was wrapped (covered in spices) and placed in a tomb, which was then sealed tight (closed up in the dough). **Read:** Matthew 27:57–60

Then Jesus was resurrected and the tomb was empty. **Read:** Matthew 28:1–9.

Empty Tomb Rolls
RECIPE

INGREDIENTS

1 can of 8 refrigerated crescent rolls

8 large marshmallows

3 tablespoons of melted butter in a shallow bowl

1 cup sugar and 2 teaspoons of cinnamon in a shallow bowl

DIRECTIONS

1. Roll out the crescent rolls and separate them onto a cookie sheet.

2. Dip each marshmallow in the butter and roll it in the cinnamon and sugar mixture, coating it evenly.

3. Place one butter and cinnamon sugar coated marshmallow on each crescent roll.

4. Pull up the narrow ends of the triangles and wrap the crescent roll dough completely around the marshmallow, sealing it well. It is important that no gaps are present.

5. Use remaining butter to brush the tops of the "tombs," and sprinkle with cinnamon sugar to taste.

6. Bake on a cookie sheet at 375°F for 14 minutes or until the tops are a deep golden brown. Cool 1 minute in the pan. Serve and enjoy!

7. When the rolls are ready to be served, have each person break their roll open to see what has happened inside. The marshmallow is gone!

That ye may have eternal life

We read about eternal life a lot in the scriptures. Eternal life means a life with no end and no beginning. Eternal life is being with our Heavenly Father and others we love. It can be hard for our brains to totally understand what eternity means.

Here is one way to help you understand eternity better: Life on earth can be represented as a line with a starting and ending point. The starting point is when you are born and the ending point on earth is when you die.

BIRTH   DEATH

Eternal life can be seen as a circle with no end and no beginning. Eternal life just keeps going and going. When someone is baptized and receives the gift of the Holy Ghost, they put themselves on a path that leads to an eternal life with our Heavenly Parents and other loved ones.

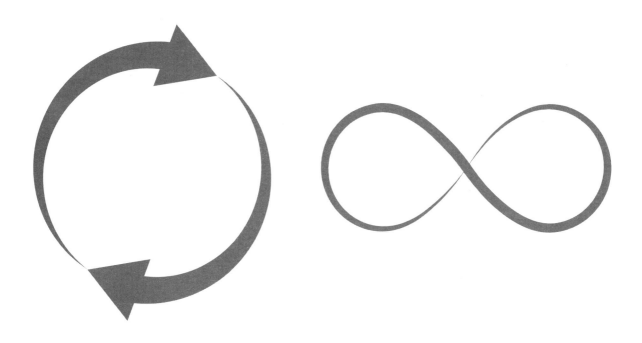

SCRIPTURES

John 3:16, Moroni 7:41, Doctrine and Covenants 14:7

Life on Earth

Look at the line below and mark where the starting and ending points are for life on earth. Now look at the circle that represents eternal life on the opposite page. Can you find a start and ending point? You cannot, because it just keeps going and going. Our eternal life is like a circle. It will just keep going and going.

Directions: See if you can find your way through the circular maze below to "Eternal Life."

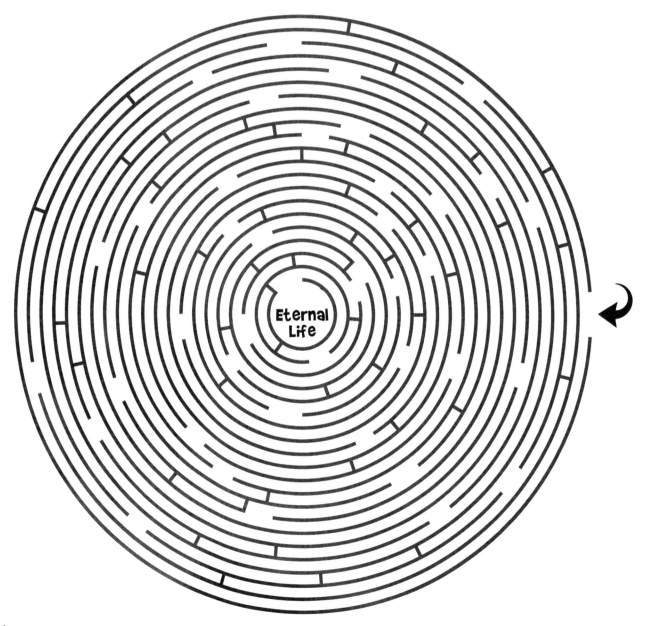

Eternity Never Ends

Directions: Pick up a small handful of sand. Do your very best to count every single piece of sand. Can you do it? It is pretty tricky. Now ask an adult to help you find a picture of the Sahara desert. Also find a picture of sand on a beach. There is no end to the sand. It is impossible to count every grain. Like the sand, eternity keeps going and going. Eternity never ends.

"I will surely do thee good, and make thy seed as the sand of the sea, which cannot be numbered." —Genesis 32:12

Directions: Place a mirror on both sides of you. Can you see an end or a beginning in the two mirrors? Just like not being able to see an end or a beginning in the mirrors, you cannot see the end or beginning of eternity. Draw a picture of your reflection in the mirror below.

That He may Pour out His Spirit more aBundantly upon you

Have you ever seen water come out of your faucet in tiny drops? If you were really thirsty and were trying to get a full cup of water one drop at a time, it would take quite a while. You would probably want to turn the faucet on all the way to fill up your cup quickly. Then you could drink the water and quench your thirst.

Heavenly Father has promised those who are baptized and follow His commandments that He will "pour out His spirit" upon them. This means that Heavenly Father covenants (promises) to give His spirit to those who are baptized and follow Him. And when He gives us this spirit, it will not be in tiny drops, but He will pour His spirit on us.

He even uses the word "abundantly." Do you know what abundantly means? Abundantly means large amounts. It is wonderful that Heavenly Father not only wants us to have His spirit with us, but He also wants us to have it in large amounts: to have His spirit poured upon us.

You may wonder, what is "His spirit?" When we read in Mosiah 13:13, the footnote teaches us that His spirit is the Holy Ghost. This means that all the wonderful things the Holy Ghost can be in our life—a comforter, protector, and so forth—can be given to us in abundance. In other words, Heavenly Father wants us to have the Holy Ghost with us to guide us, not in small portions, but in large amounts. This is a gift from Him to us.

SCRIPTURES

Mosiah 13:13, John 14:26, Acts 2:38,
Doctrine and Covenants 8:2–3

Having His Spirit in Abundance

Directions: Find a cup and take it to your sink. Turn the water on so that it runs as little as possible. (See if you can get it to run only in drops.) Time how long it takes you to fill up your cup this way and write it here. _____

Now, turn the water on in a full stream. Time how long it takes to fill up your cup this way (abundantly) and write it here. _____

Question: What does this exercise teach you about having things in abundance?

Answer: _____

Question: How does it make you feel that Heavenly Father wants you to have His spirit poured upon you abundantly?

Answer: _____

Questions You Might Have: _____

_____

_____

_____

What Does it mean to have a testimony of God and Jesus Christ?

WHAT IS A TESTIMONY?

A testimony is when you know and bear witness that something is true. Gospel truths are taught to you and a testimony of them is given to you by the Spirit. Some of the most important parts of your testimony include believing that

1. Heavenly Father and Jesus Christ live.

2. Heavenly Father and Jesus Christ love all of the children on the earth, including YOU.

3. Jesus Christ atoned for our sins. This means Jesus made it possible for us to be forgiven for the mistakes we make so we can try again.

SCRIPTURES

Alma 32:27, Alma 5:45–46

Building Your Testimony

Directions: All good buildings must have a foundation. Gather some blocks together to build a building.

Begin your building with a foundation. As you add blocks to your foundation, compare this to building your testimony. For example, as you add one block to your foundation, it might represent a part of your testimony that knows Jesus Christ loves you. Another block may represent that you feel happy when you pray. Keep adding blocks as you share parts of your testimony until your building is complete.

Directions: It is important to have a good foundation to build your testimony on, just like a building needs a good foundation. Can you draw a building below by adding your own blocks to the foundation provided?

Parts of Your Own Testimony

Directions: Look at the blocks below. On each block, write something that is a part of your testimony.

Growing Your Testimony

Your testimony will grow throughout your life. Just like a garden grows.

Directions: Look at the garden below. It needs more flowers. Can you add more flowers to it? On each flower, write something that can be a part of your testimony. You can also ask your parents, other family members, and Primary teachers what some of the parts of their testimony are. Draw more flowers in your garden and add their ideas to them.

GOD IS OUR HEAVENLY FATHER

A song many children love to sing is, "I am a child of God" (*Hymns*, no. 301). In the words to this song, we learn how special God is. We also learn that we are God's children. God is your Heavenly Father.

God created the entire earth. He created you and all the other people on the earth. God is the smartest person ever. He knows all things. God is perfect. The most important thing to know about God is that He loves you. God loves all of us. He wants us to learn and grow. God wants us to come back to live with Him someday.

We sing a hymn called, "O My Father" (*Hymns*, no. 292). A few lines from this hymn read, "In the heav'ns are parents single? No, the thought makes reason stare! Truth is reason; truth eternal tells me I've a mother there."

This song can help us remember that our Heavenly Parents love us very much.

SCRIPTURES

Malachi 2:10, Matthew 3:13–17, Mosiah 4:9,
Doctrine and Covenants 130:22

GOD'S LoVe

Directions: Read the following scriptures about God's love. As you read them, choose words in them that teach you what God's love means to you, and draw or write them in the hearts below.

Psalm 36:7

Romans 8:35–39

1 John 4:7–8

Matthew 19:14–15

Eleventh Article of Faith

Directions: Complete the word search below by finding the bolded words in this article of faith.

11 We **claim** the **privilege** of **worshiping** **Almighty** **God** **according** to the **dictates** of our own **conscience**, and **allow** all **men** the **same** privilege, let them worship **how**, **where**, or **what** they may.

```
A C C O R D I N G A G O D Q H
K W G A P V I V K L L B Y D O
V W D A Q Z K U H L N S H Y W
W R I Z C H V Y C O T P F O E
H I C W A L K O E W C R U H I
A Q T V A Y A A P K O S X H Q
T X A D M W G I U S N P Z A M
X I T J R A J K M A S K E E H
Y H E E Q X O G N M C U Y W Y
U M S H P S M H N E I I V O O
T E E H S R X P Y F E G S R Y
N C F N J L I S F Z N T F S Q
X J W J Q Q K V M O C A Z H V
P J S L O D L R I H E P O I J
S S W H E R E V E L B R F P U
A U L G L X O M P X E P B I P
U A L M I G H T Y M W G J N F
P J R W V K O S X H B H E G V
Z F A D C L K V C S S G X T J
G D U Z K I I X W F N W P J R
```

Heavenly Parents

Directions: Read the poem below by Eliza R. Snow. It is called, "My Father in Heaven." You may recognize it from the hymn "O My Father."

**"In the heav'ns are parents single?
No, the thought makes reason stare; Truth is reason—truth eternal
Tells me I've a mother there."[1]**

Question: What does this poem teach you about your Heavenly Parents?

Answer: _____

_____

_____

_____

_____

_____

_____

1. "My Father in Heaven," in "Poetry, for the Times and Seasons," *Times and Seasons* 6 (Nov. 15, 1845): 1039; "O My Father," *Hymns*, no. 292. See also Jill Mulvay Derr, "The Significance of 'O My Father' in the Personal Journey of Eliza R. Snow," *BYU Studies* 36, no. 1 (1996–97), 84–126.

Jesus Christ is the Son of God

Jesus Christ is God's son. All of the things that Jesus did point us back to God. When we follow Jesus, it is easier to know God.

Jesus Christ died for us. Because He died for us, we can have mercy in our lives. Mercy means we can be forgiven when we make mistakes. After Jesus died, He was resurrected. This means that Jesus lives. Because Jesus lives, we can all live again after we die. These things that Jesus did for us are called the Atonement.

SCRIPTURES

1 Timothy 2:5, 1 Nephi 22:12, Alma 5:48,
Doctrine & Covenants 45:3, "The Living Christ" (*Ensign*, Apr. 2000)

Jesus Christ and God

Jesus Christ and God have other names. This can sometimes be confusing. It makes it difficult to know who we are talking about. Below is a chart you can color that gives some of the other names God and Jesus Christ are known by.

GOD	JESUS CHRIST
Heavenly Father	Savior
God the Father	Son of God
Supreme Being	Redeemer
Elohim	Prince of Peace
Father in Heaven	Only Begotten of the Father
Heavenly Parent	Mediator
	Advocate
	Christ
	Jehovah
	Jesus
	Lord
	Emmanuel
	Counsellor
	Messiah
	King of Kings

Third Article of Faith

Directions: Color this article of faith then cut it out and hang it somewhere you will see it each day.

The Third Article of Faith

We believe that through the Atonement of Christ, all mankind may be saved, by obedience to the laws and ordinances of the Gospel.

The Living Christ

THE TESTIMONY OF THE APOSTLES

THE CHURCH OF JESUS CHRIST OF LATTER-DAY SAINTS

As we commemorate the birth of Jesus Christ two millennia ago, we offer our testimony of the reality of His matchless life and the infinite virtue of His great atoning sacrifice. None other has had so profound an influence upon all who have lived and will yet live upon the earth.

He was the Great Jehovah of the Old Testament, the Messiah of the New. Under the direction of His Father, He was the creator of the earth. "All things were made by him; and without him was not any thing made that was made" (John 1:3). Though sinless, He was baptized to fulfill all righteousness. He "went about doing good" (Acts 10:38), yet was despised for it. His gospel was a message of peace and goodwill. He entreated all to follow His example. He walked the roads of Palestine, healing the sick, causing the blind to see, and raising the dead. He taught the truths of eternity, the reality of our premortal existence, the purpose of our life on earth, and the potential for the sons and daughters of God in the life to come.

He instituted the sacrament as a reminder of His great atoning sacrifice. He was arrested and condemned on spurious charges, convicted to satisfy a mob, and sentenced to die on Calvary's cross. He gave His life to atone for the sins of all mankind. His was a great vicarious gift in behalf of all who would ever live upon the earth.

We solemnly testify that His life, which is central to all human history, neither began in Bethlehem nor concluded on Calvary. He was the Firstborn of the Father, the Only Begotten Son in the flesh, the Redeemer of the world.

He rose from the grave to "become the firstfruits of them that slept" (1 Cor. 15:20). As Risen Lord, He visited among those He had loved in life. He also ministered among His "other sheep" (John 10:16) in ancient America. In the modern world, He and His Father appeared to the boy Joseph Smith, ushering in the long-promised "dispensation of the fulness of times" (Eph. 1:10).

Of the Living Christ, the Prophet Joseph wrote: "His eyes were as a flame of fire; the hair of his head was white like the pure snow; his countenance shone above the brightness of the sun; and his voice was as the sound of the rushing of great waters, even the voice of Jehovah, saying:

"I am the first and the last; I am he who liveth, I am he who was slain; I am your advocate with the Father" (D&C 110:3–4).

Of Him the Prophet also declared: "And now, after the many testimonies which have been given of him, this is the testimony, last of all, which we give of him: That he lives!

"For we saw him, even on the right hand of God; and we heard the voice bearing record that he is the Only Begotten of the Father—

"That by him, and through him, and of him, the worlds are and were created, and the inhabitants thereof are begotten sons and daughters unto God" (D&C 76:22–24).

We declare in words of solemnity that His priesthood and His Church have been restored upon the earth—"built upon the foundation of . . . apostles and prophets, Jesus Christ himself being the chief corner stone" (Eph. 2:20).

We testify that He will someday return to earth. "And the glory of the Lord shall be revealed, and all flesh shall see it together" (Isa. 40:5). He will rule as King of Kings and reign as Lord of Lords, and every knee shall bend and every tongue shall speak in worship before Him. Each of us will stand to be judged of Him according to our works and the desires of our hearts.

We bear testimony, as His duly ordained Apostles—that Jesus is the Living Christ, the immortal Son of God. He is the great King Immanuel, who stands today on the right hand of His Father. He is the light, the life, and the hope of the world. His way is the path that leads to happiness in this life and eternal life in the world to come. God be thanked for the matchless gift of His divine Son.

What Does it mean that the gospel of Jesus Christ has Been restored through the Prophet Joseph Smith?

WHAT IS THE GOSPEL OF JESUS CHRIST?

The gospel is often referred to as Heavenly Father's plan of happiness. Some people refer to the gospel as the "good news" from Heavenly Father. The gospel can help us live a happy life—a life that will one day lead to us to live with Heavenly Father forever.

IMPORTANT PARTS OF THE GOSPEL INCLUDE

1. Believing that God loves us and will guide us as we ask for His help (faith)

2. Being forgiven when we make mistakes (repentance)

3. Choosing to be baptized to show Heavenly Father that we believe Him and want to follow Him

4. Receiving the gift of the Holy Ghost. The Holy Ghost guides us in choosing between right and wrong and knowing what Heavenly Father would want us to do.

Directions: Below is a drawing of a dove, but the drawing is not finished. Can you finish drawing the dove? What does the dove symbolize?

SCRIPTURES

Articles of Faith 1:4, Doctrine and Covenants 39:5–6, Romans 1:16–17, Alma 32:26–29

Read all about it!

Directions: The gospel is often referred to as the "good news." Below is a newspaper. Write a headline you could use to tell people about the good news of the gospel. Then use the space below your headline to draw or write parts of the gospel that are good news to you.

NEWS

Edition 012345

1

Fourth Article of Faith

Directions: Using only the first initial of each word from the fourth article of faith, see if you can recite it:

W b t t f p a o t G a f F

i t L J C s R t B b i f t r o

s f L o o h f t g o t H G

Repentance

Directions: Hold the message below up to a mirror to help you decode which article of faith it is. Once you've decoded it, set a timer for 60 seconds and see how many times you can read it in that time. Can you beat your score if you try again?

We Believe that men will be
punished for their own sins, and
not for Adam's transgression.

Plant a Seed

Alma teaches us that faith is like a seed (Alma 32:26-29).

Directions: Get a cup, some dirt, a few seeds (the following seeds grow quickly: sunflowers, radishes, beans, marigolds, and cherry tomatoes), and some water.

Step 1. Fill a cup ¾ of the way full with dirt.

Step 2. Place your seed on the dirt in the cup.

Step 3. Barely cover your seed with the dirt.

Step 4. Add about a tablespoon of water every other day and watch your seed grow.

Step 5. Record your observations below of what your seed is doing each day.

DAY 1	DAY 2
DAY 3	DAY 4
DAY 5	DAY 6
DAY 7	DAY 8

Question: How can your testimony grow like this seed is growing?

Answer: _____

_____

Question: What helps your testimony grow? Can the water be like reading your scriptures? Is the sun like going to church or saying your prayers?

Answer: _____

_____

Why Did the gospel of Jesus Christ need to Be restored?

To restore something means to bring something back. For example, sometimes people can take an old couch that has been scratched or ripped and restore it. They restore it by fixing the scratches and tears. They make the couch like new again.

OLD & TORN

RESTORED

After Jesus died, many important and precious parts of the true church became lost or were altered (changed) so they were no longer true. Followers of Jesus were often punished for saying good things about Him and His gospel. This time in our history was not happy, and many people did not know about God and Jesus Christ.

Like the broken chair, what people knew about the true church and God were broken. God's truths and His Church needed to be restored or brought back to the way they were supposed to be. Bringing these truths back is called the restoration of the gospel.

The Church was restored by the prophet Joseph Smith. Some important things that were restored included the priesthood and temple ordinances. Joseph Smith also translated the Book of Mormon, which contains the pure gospel of Jesus Christ.

SCRIPTURES

2 Nephi 3:3–15, Joseph Smith—History 1:68–72

Restoring the Gospel

Directions: Go to a secondhand store or look around your home to find something that is broken or worn out. See what you can do to restore it.

For example, you could take a book that has some ripped pages and tape the pages back together again. Share what you did with your family and talk about what it means to restore something. Then you can share with them what you learned about the gospel being restored and write it below.

Who is Joseph Smith and how did he restore the gospel of Jesus Christ?

As a young boy, Joseph Smith would read the Bible. One day he read **James 1:5, "If any of ye lack wisdom, let him ask of God."** This scripture was very special to Joseph Smith. At the time, Joseph had been wondering which church he should join. After reading this in the Bible, Joseph knew he needed to ask God which church was true.

Joseph decided to go to a forest area that we now call the Sacred Grove. Joseph knelt and prayed. Joseph asked God which church he should join. Heavenly Father and Jesus Christ appeared to Joseph Smith. They told Joseph he was not supposed to join any of the churches.

Joseph continued to listen to Heavenly Father and Jesus and do what they asked him to do. Because of this, They called him to be a prophet and restore the gospel of Jesus Christ.

Question: What does it mean to restore something?

Answer: _____

_____

_____

Question: List items in your home that have been restored or need to be restored.

Answer: _____

_____

_____

SCRIPTURES

Doctrine & Covenants 21:1–15, Joseph Smith—History 1

Amazing things happened to Joseph Smith

Directions: Color and write in the box next to each picture the order that each scene happened to help Joseph Smith restore the gospel of Jesus Christ.

Seventh Article of Faith

Directions: The article of faith below is missing some words. The missing words have images where the words should be. What does this article of faith say? Copy the words onto the lines at the bottom of this page and add the correct words in place of the images.

We Believe in the [gift]
of [tongue], Prophecy,
revelation, [eyes],
[bandage], interpretation
of [tongues], and so forth.

_____

_____

_____

_____

_____

Ninth Article of Faith

Directions: Color this article of faith then cut it out and hang it somewhere you will see it each day.

The Ninth Article of Faith

We believe all that God has revealed, all that He does now reveal, and we believe that He will yet reveal many great and important things pertaining to the kingdom of God.

The Book of Mormon is another testament of Jesus Christ

When you look at the title page of the Book of Mormon, you can see the full name of this precious book of scripture. Its full name is "The Book of Mormon: Another Testament of Jesus Christ."

Can you think of another important book that testifies of Jesus Christ? If you're thinking of the Bible, you are right. The Bible testifies of Christ. This means it teaches about Jesus Christ. It helps us know who Jesus Christ is and that He came to earth to show us how we can have joy and find peace. It teaches that everything Jesus did was to lead us to Heavenly Father and show us what we must do to one day return to Him.

Like the Bible, the Book of Mormon testifies of Jesus Christ. It is another testament of Jesus Christ. Jesus Christ is such an important part of the Book of Mormon that Heavenly Father wanted to make sure He was included in the title. Jesus Christ is talked about throughout the entire Book of Mormon.

We can read in the introduction to the Book of Mormon about one of the most important events in history. This is when Christ came to teach the Nephites after He was resurrected. Jesus Christ is a very important part of the Book of Mormon.

SCRIPTURES

Isaiah 29:11–14, Ezekiel 37:15–17, 1 Nephi 13:38–41,
Doctrine and Covenants 20:8–12, Title page of the Book of
Mormon, Introduction to the Book of Mormon

Book of Mormon
— READING CHART —

A daily habit of scripture study will strengthen your faith and help you receive personal inspiration and guidance. If you read just five minutes a day, you can complete the entire Book of Mormon in one year. Color in each chapter after you read it.

1ST NEPHI (1) (2) (3) (4) (5) (6) (7) (8) (9) (10) (11) (12) (13)
(14) (15) (16) (17) (18) (19) (20) (21) (22) 2ND NEPHI (1) (2) (3) (4)
(5) (6) (7) (8) (9) (10) (11) (12) (13) (14) (15) (16) (17) (18) (19) (20)
(21) (22) (23) (24) (25) (26) (27) (28) (29) (30) (31) (32) (33) JACOB (1)
(2) (3) (4) (5) (6) (7) ENOS (1) JAROM (1) OMNI (1)
WORDS OF MORMON (1) MOSIAH (1) (2) (3) (4) (5) (6)
(7) (8) (9) (10) (11) (12) (13) (14) (15) (16) (17) (18) (19) (20) (21) (22)
(23) (24) (25) (26) (27) (28) (29) ALMA (1) (2) (3) (4) (5) (6) (7)
(8) (9) (10) (11) (12) (13) (14) (15) (16) (17) (18) (19) (20) (21) (22) (23)
(24) (25) (26) (27) (28) (29) (30) (31) (32) (33) (34) (35) (36) (37) (38) (39)
(40) (41) (42) (43) (44) (45) (46) (47) (48) (49) (50) (51) (52) (53) (54) (55)
(56) (57) (58) (59) (60) (61) (62) (63) HELAMAN (1) (2) (3) (4) (5)
(6) (7) (8) (9) (10) (11) (12) (13) (14) (15) (16) 3RD NEPHI (1) (2)
(3) (4) (5) (6) (7) (8) (9) (10) (11) (12) (13) (14) (15) (16) (17) (18)
(19) (20) (21) (22) (23) (24) (25) (26) (27) (28) (29) (30) 4TH NEPHI (1)
MORMON (1) (2) (3) (4) (5) (6) (7) (8) (9) ETHER (1) (2)
(3) (4) (5) (6) (7) (8) (9) (10) (11) (12) (13) (14) (15) MORONI
(1) (2) (3) (4) (5) (6) (7) (8) (9) (10) YOU'VE FINISHED!

Eighth Article of Faith

Directions: Complete the word search below by finding the bolded words in this article of faith.

We **believe** the **Bible** to be the **word** of **God** as far as it is **translated correctly**; we also believe the **Book of Mormon** to be the word of God.

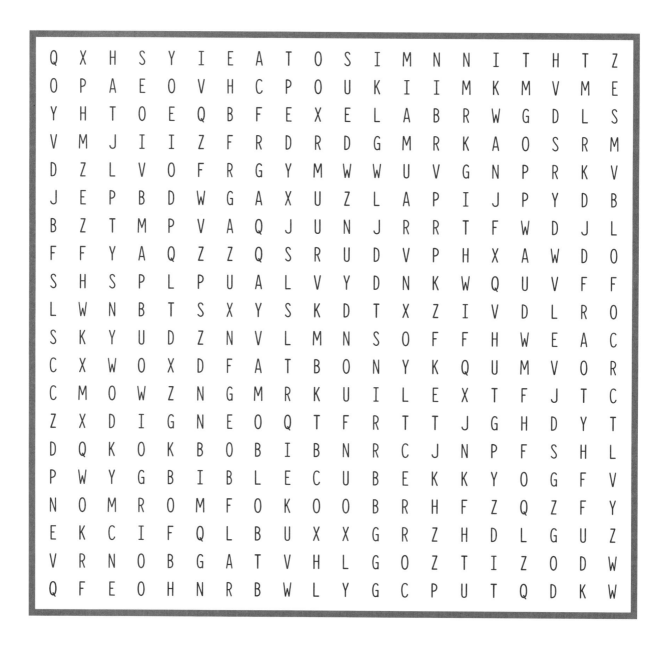

What Does it mean to Be Confirmed and receive the gift of the Holy Ghost?

WHAT DOES IT MEAN TO BE CONFIRMED?

After you are baptized, you will be confirmed. You will be asked to sit in a chair. Men holding the priesthood will stand in a circle around you. Each of the men will place one hand on your head and one hand on the shoulder of the man standing next to him.

The person you asked to confirm you will then begin to speak. He may say some nice things about you and your purposes on this earth. This part of the blessing can be different with each person, but every confirmation must include these things:

1. The name of the person being confirmed

2. That the ordinance (confirmation) is being performed by the authority of the Melchizedek Priesthood

3. Confirmation that the person is now a member of The Church of Jesus Christ of Latter-day Saints

4. Declaration to the individual to "receive the Holy Ghost"

5. Ending with, "In the name of Jesus Christ"

SCRIPTURES

Acts 2:38, Act 8:12–17, Acts 19: 1–6

Being Confirmed

Directions: Color this picture of a child being confirmed.

Question: What are three things you notice that are happening in this picture?

Answer: _____

_____

_____

Memories of Being Confirmed

Directions: Ask an adult you trust what they remember about being confirmed. Use the space provided below to write some of the things you learned from talking to them.

Question: Who do you want to confirm you?

Answer: _____

Question: How do you know this person?

Answer: _____

Question: What questions do you still have about being confirmed?

Answer: _____

_____

Who is the Holy Ghost?

The Holy Ghost works with Heavenly Father and Jesus Christ in what is called the Godhead. The Holy Ghost does not have a body. He is a spirit.

The Holy Ghost will act as a witness in your life to help you understand the difference between right and wrong. He can warn you if you are in danger.

> *A young man was driving down the road when the Holy Ghost told him to "STOP!" This young man listened to the Holy Ghost and stopped. Just as he stopped, a big car sped past him from the other direction. Listening to the Holy Ghost kept this young man safe.*

The Holy Ghost can also be a comforter. This means that the Holy Ghost can comfort you or bring you relief from things that might be making you sad, worried, or scared.

Have you ever wrapped yourself in a soft, fluffy blanket? Being wrapped in a blanket can feel so nice. Another word for blanket is comforter. Just as the blanket can help you feel comfort and warmth, the Holy Ghost can provide you with comfort to ease your concerns.

SCRIPTURES

1 Nephi 10:17–19, 2 Nephi 31:18, Moroni 10:5, John 14:26, Doctrine and Covenants 130:22, Articles of Faith 1:1

Directions: Read the story from the January 2018 *Friend* magazine called "An Answer for Lucia" (media.ldscdn.org/pdf/magazines/friend-january-2018/2018-01-21-an -answer-for-lucia-eng.pdf). Then answer the following questions about what you read. Write your answers in the spaces provided below or talk about the answers with someone.

Question: What was Lucia sad about?

Answer: _____

Question: What did the teacher say when she looked at Lucia that made everyone laugh?

Answer: _____

Question: What was Lucia confused about?

Answer: _____

Question: Who did Lucia know that she could talk to and ask for help in finding answers to her questions?

Answer: _____

Question: Are Heavenly Father, Jesus Christ, and the Holy Ghost separate people?

Answer: _____

Question: What were some scriptures the missionaries shared with Lucia that taught that Heavenly Father, Jesus Christ, and the Holy Ghost are separate?

Answer: _____

Question: What scripture did the missionaries use to help Lucia when she asked, "So why do those other scriptures say they are the same?"

Answer: _____

Question: What helped Lucia feel warm inside and know that what the missionaries taught was true?

Answer: _____

Jesus was Baptized

The scripture below talks about when Jesus was baptized. Each member of the Godhead was present at Jesus's baptism.

Directions: Read the scripture below and identify each member of the Godhead by

1. **Putting a circle around Jesus's name.**

2. **Putting a box around the words "Spirit of God" (the Holy Ghost).**

3. **Underlining "a voice from heaven, saying, This is my beloved Son" (Heavenly Father).**

Doing this will help you see where each member of the Godhead is represented in this scripture and at Jesus's baptism.

And Jesus, when he was baptized, went up straightway out of the water: and, lo, the heavens were opened unto him, and he saw the Spirit of God descending like a dove, and lighting upon him: And lo a voice from heaven, saying, This is my beloved Son, in whom I am well pleased.

—Matthew 3:16–17

The Holy Ghost

Directions: Fill in the missing words to the first article of faith that teaches us about the Godhead. After filling in the words, see if you can memorize the article of faith and say it to a member of your family.

"We believe in_____ , the Eternal_____ , and in His

_____ , Jesus _____ , and in the _____ _____ ."

Missing words: Father, God, Ghost, Christ, Holy, son

The Holy Ghost is also called the comforter because He can provide comfort to us when we need it. Another word for blanket is comforter.

Directions: Use your creativity to draw and design a comforter in the space provided. Then answer the questions below.

Question: Do you have a favorite blanket that you like to use?

Answer: _____

Question: What makes this blanket more comfortable to you?

Answer: _____

Question: How can the Holy Ghost be a comforter to you?

Answer: _____

What Does it mean to receive the gift of the Holy Ghost?

The gift of the Holy Ghost is having the "constant companionship of the Holy Ghost." This means that as we try to do what is right, the Holy Ghost is always with us.

The Holy Ghost can help all people. When we are baptized and confirmed, we are given a special blessing to have the gift of the Holy Ghost.

Have you ever seen the movie Peter Pan? When Peter meets Wendy he is crying. Do you remember why Peter is crying? Peter is sad because he keeps losing his shadow. Wendy offers to sew his shadow to his foot so he will always know where it is. Peter is so happy about always knowing where his shadow is that he bounces around the room and sings the song, "I've gotta crow!"

When you receive the gift of the Holy Ghost, it will mean that you will have the blessing of always having the Holy Ghost with you. The Holy Ghost will help you whenever you need Him. The thought of always being able to have the Holy Ghost with you just might make you want to bounce around with joy and sing like Peter Pan did when he was able to have his shadow with him all the time.

SCRIPTURES

2 Nephi 31:12–17, Doctrine and Covenants 8:2–3, Doctrine and Covenants 68:25–28, Doctrine and Covenants 121:46

The Gift of the Holy Ghost

Directions: There are four gift boxes below. Write something on each gift box that we can receive from having the gift of the Holy Ghost in our lives. Some ideas can include comfort, truth, companionship, and peace. Color each gift box after you have written something on it.

The Holy Ghost Comforts You

Directions: Look up the following scriptures and fill in the missing words. You can also color the image below of the girl being comforted by her blanket much like the Holy Ghost comforts you.

Doctrine and Covenants 121:46: "The Holy Ghost shall be thy constant _____ , and thy scepter an unchanging scepter of righteousness and _____ ; and thy dominion shall be an everlasting dominion, and without compulsory means it shall flow unto thee _____ and ever."

2 Nephi 31:12: "And also, the voice of the _____ came unto me, saying: He that is _____ in my name, to him will the Father give the _____ _____ , like unto me; wherefore, _____ me, and do the things which ye have seen me do."

77

What is tithing and what does it mean to pay tithing?

Tithing is when someone takes a tenth part of what they have earned and gives it to the Lord. For example, let's say you were to do some work and earn ten dollars. A tenth of those ten dollars would be one dollar.

If you chose to pay tithing, you would take one dollar and pay it to the Church and keep the remaining nine dollars for yourself.

You can pay tithing by getting a gray envelope from outside your bishop's office, along with a form to fill out. Your parents can help you fill out the form. You will place the form in the envelope with your one dollar. Once your tithing is inside the envelope, you can hand it to a member of your bishopric.

It is a blessing to pay tithing. We are blessed when we pay tithing. Tithing dollars are used for things like building churches and temples, helping missionaries, and building the kingdom of God on earth.

$1.00 FOR TITHING

$9.00 FOR YOURSELF

SCRIPTURES

Genesis 14:18–20, Malachi 3:8–11, D&C 119

understanding a tenth

A tenth is what we have been asked to give for tithing. A tithe represents a tenth.

Lay out ten coins or other items such as grapes, candy, rocks, and so forth. Count the items to make sure you have ten. Place the items in a row.

Take one piece from the row and place it to the side. Point to the one item and say, "This tenth is what I will give for tithing, because a tithe represents a tenth." Repeat this exercise with different items.

Directions: There are ten donuts below. Color nine of the ten donuts to show how many you would keep, and leave one donut uncolored to represent the tenth, or the tithe you would pay to the church.

Paying tithing

Would you like an opportunity to pay tithing? Ask your parents if there is something you can do to earn ten dimes. Once you've earned your ten dimes, hold onto them until Sunday. Remember, a tithe is one tenth, so you will only need to take one dime to church to pay your tithing with.

On Sunday when you go to church, go to your bishop's office. Outside of his office, pick up a donation form and an envelope. Ask an adult to help you fill out the form. Put the form in the envelope along with your tithing (a dime). Take your tithing to a member of the bishopric.

Directions: Below are 10 coins, a tithing envelope, and a piggy bank. Color the images. Cut out the coins and glue what you would give for tithing onto the envelope. Next, glue the coins you would keep onto the piggy bank.

What is the Word of Wisdom and what does it mean to follow the Word of Wisdom?

The Word of Wisdom can be viewed as rules to help us keep our bodies healthy. The Lord gave us these rules to help us be healthy. Being healthy also benefits our spirits.

We can read about the Word of Wisdom in Doctrine and Covenants section 89. This section of scripture teaches us that the Lord revealed foods that are good for us to eat. The Lord also taught us things that are not good for our bodies. When we obey the Word of Wisdom, we live safer lives and have better health, knowledge, and wisdom.

SCRIPTURES

D&C 89:5–21, D&C 89:5–7, D&C 89:8, D&C 89:9, D&C 89:10–11,
D&C 89:12–13, D&C 89:14–17, D&C 89:18–21

It's a Blessing to have a Body

Directions: Using a timer, see how many things you can say about your body in 30 seconds, such as, "My body can walk for a long time," or "My body can eat yummy food."

When you are done, review with an adult or other family members some of the ideas you came up with. Write a few of your favorites below.

_____

_____

_____

_____

MY BODY

The Word of Wisdom can help you care for your Body

It is a great blessing to have a body. Our bodies are a gift from Heavenly Father, and He wants us to take good care of this gift. Our Heavenly Father has given us the Word of Wisdom to help us care for our bodies.

Directions: Look at the images below of a happy face and a frowning face. Read the Word of Wisdom and find those things that are good for your body and those that are not good for your body. When you find something that is good, draw a picture of it or write the word under the smiley face. When you find something that is not good, draw a picture of it or write the word under the frowning face.

What is the Sabbath Day?

The Sabbath day is often referred to as the Lord's day. The Sabbath day is observed every week on Sunday. There are many things we do throughout the week. The Sabbath day should be different than the other days of the week.

Heavenly Father has asked that the Sabbath day be a day set aside for us to focus on rest and worship. To focus means to give our attention to something. When we use the Sabbath day to focus on rest, it means that we take a break from things we may typically do. This allows our bodies and minds to have a break.

For example, if I were a runner, I could choose to not run on the Sabbath to give my body a rest from something I typically do on the other days of the week. One way I could focus my time on worship on the Sabbath day would be to attend my church meetings.

President Russell M. Nelson taught, "I learned from the scriptures that my conduct and my attitude on the Sabbath constituted a sign between me and my Heavenly Father. With that understanding, I no longer needed lists of dos and don'ts. When I had to make a decision whether or not an activity was appropriate for the Sabbath, I simply asked myself, 'What sign do I want to give to God?' That question made my choices about the Sabbath day crystal clear" ("The Sabbath Is a Delight," *Ensign*, May 2015).

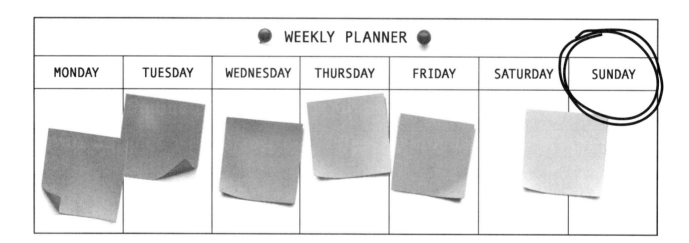

SCRIPTURES

Exodus 20:8–11, Matthew 12:9–13, Luke 4:16, John 5:9,
Doctrine and Covenants 59:9–10

God's People have always observed the Sabbath Day

Directions: With an adult's help, read Genesis 1–2. These chapters teach about the creation of the earth. Pause at each day and draw or write some of the things that occurred that day in each square on the next four pages.

For example:

DAY ONE, draw a circle and shade in half of the circle with black. Leave the other half white to indicate night and day (Genesis 1:3–5).

DAY TWO, draw some clouds to represent the firmament of heaven (Genesis 1:6–8).

DAY THREE, draw some flowers or plants to represent the plants of the earth (Genesis 1:9–13).

DAY FOUR, draw a sun, moon, and stars to represent the greater lights to rule the day and the lesser light to rule the night (Genesis 1:14–19).

DAY FIVE, draw a bird and a fish to represent the fowls in the sky and the fishes in the sea (Genesis 1:20–23).

DAY SIX, draw some animals to represent the living creatures on the land. Also draw a picture of a man and a woman to represent Adam and Eve being created in God's image (Genesis 1:24–31).

DAY SEVEN, draw a picture of a chair or bed to represent that on this day, God rested (Genesis 2:1–3).

After you have gone through and discussed what happened on each day, notice what happened on the seventh day. The seventh day is also known as Sunday or the Sabbath. God set an example for us by resting on the seventh day or on the Sabbath day. God's people continue to keep the Sabbath day holy.

Day 1 of the creation

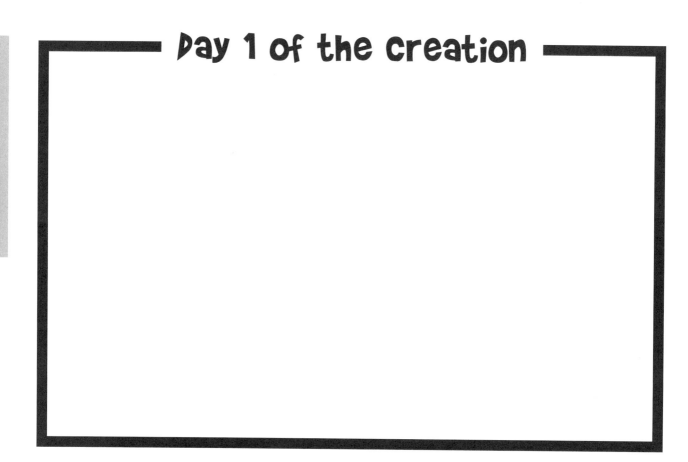

Day 2 of the creation

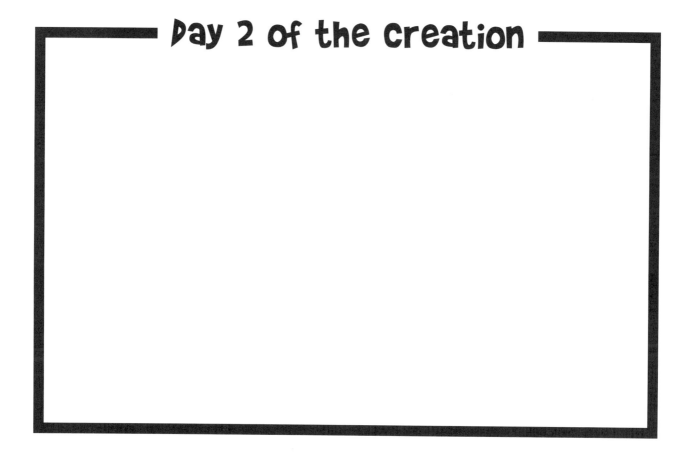

Day 3 of the Creation

Day 4 of the Creation

Day 5 of the Creation

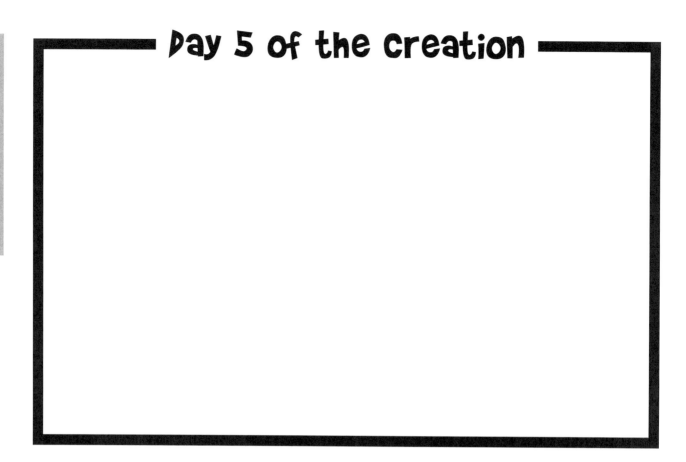

Day 6 of the Creation

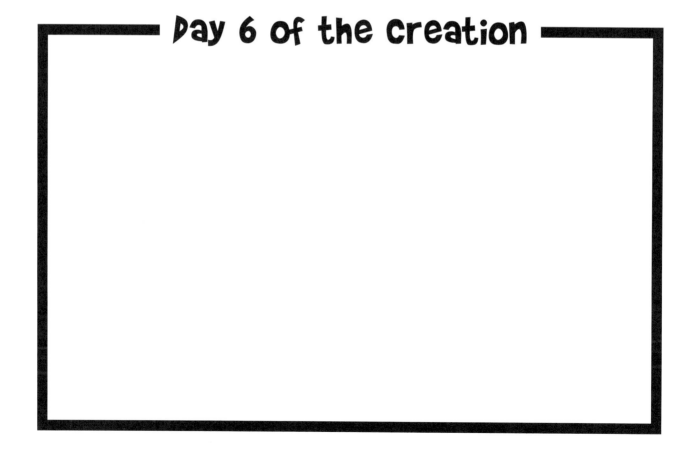

Day 7 of the Creation

What is the law of chastity?

When we obey the law of chastity, we are respectful to our body and to other peoples' bodies. We can show respect to our bodies and other people's bodies by thinking good thoughts and using kind words when we talk about bodies. We follow the law of chastity when we are appropriate in how we touch our body and other peoples' bodies.

Directions: On the shield below, draw and color pictures or write words that show how you can live the law of chastity.

SCRIPTURES

Alma 38:12, 1 Corinthians 6:19–20, Exodus 20:14

Love your Body!

Directions: Using butcher paper and a crayon, or chalk outside on a sidewalk, have someone trace the outline of your body. Look at the outline of your body. Think of at least three things to say about what you like about your body.

For example: You could include, "Look at how tall my body is." Remember that part of following the law of chastity is to have nice thoughts and words about our body and other peoples' bodies.

You can use the lines below to list more things that you like about your body.

_____

_____

_____

_____

_____

_____

_____

_____

_____

_____

Point out different parts of your body.[1]

You may have more questions about chastity. Find an adult you trust and talk to them about your questions.

1. "Talking to children frankly but reverently and using the correct names for the parts and functions of their bodies will help them grow up without unnecessary embarrassment about their bodies" (*Gospels Principles*, lesson 39, page 225; see also churchofjesuschrist.org).

What is repentance?

Repentance is a wonderful gift that we can use as often as we need to. We can even use the gift of repentance many times in one day. When we realize we have done something wrong, we can turn to our Heavenly Father. We can let Him know that we recognize we have made a bad choice and then ask Him to forgive us. We can make a promise that we will try our best to do better next time.

I remember breaking one of my Grandma's favorite plates. I felt so bad that I even cried when I had to tell her what I had done. I said I was sorry. My Grandma looked at me. She knew I was sorry. She gave me a big hug and said that it was okay and I didn't need to feel sad about it anymore. Being forgiven and able to try again is, in a small way, what it's like for Jesus to make wrong things right again.

Heavenly Father loves us. He will forgive us and help us do better. When we repent, we do not need to keep worrying about the mistakes we have made. We can learn from what we have done and continue each day to do better.

SCRIPTURES

Proverbs 28:13, Luke 15:7, 3 Nephi 9:13–14,
Doctrine and Covenants 58:42–43

steps of repentance

There is not an exact way to repent, but the following steps may help you as you learn to repent.

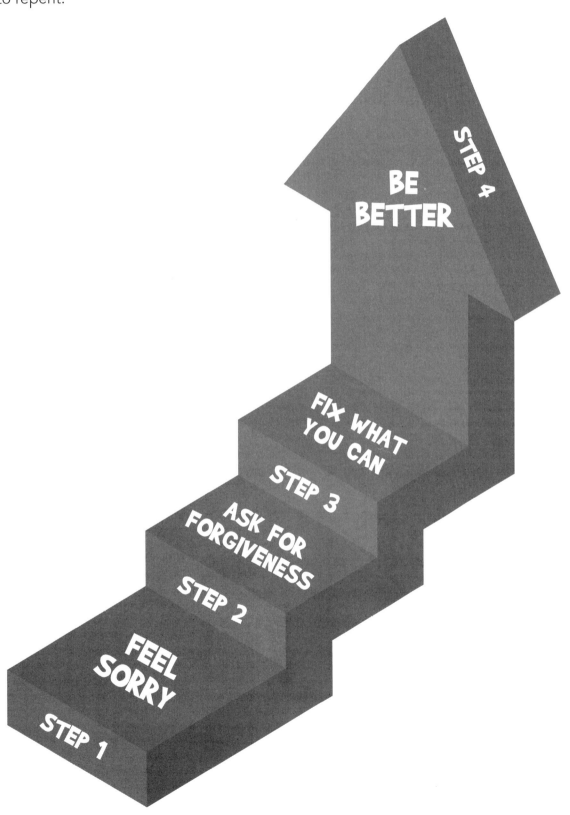

Using the Steps of Repentance

Ali was in the store with her mom when she saw some candy that she really wanted. She asked her mom if she could have the candy. Her mom said, "No. It is almost dinner time." Ali was sad because she wanted the candy.

Ali decided to put the candy in her pocket and not tell her mom. When they got home, Ali ran to her room to eat the yummy candy. Not long after Ali ate the candy, she began to feel bad. She realized she was not telling her mom the truth. She also realized by putting the candy in her pocket and not paying for it, she had stolen the piece of candy. Ali did not like how she was feeling.

Directions: Let's use the steps of repentance to see how Ali can start to feel better.

Feel Sorry: Ali is already feeling sorry. "Not long after Ali ate the candy, she began to feel bad."

Ask for forgiveness: Ali should ask for forgiveness from at least two people. Can you think of who those two people are and write the answer below?

_____

Fix What You Can: What is something Ali could do to help fix the wrong she did in stealing the piece of candy?

_____

Be Better: What is something Ali could do next time she is in the store to show that she is trying to do better?

_____

Third Article of Faith

Directions: Complete the puzzle by filling in all of the underlined words from the third article of faith below. The word *ordinances* is already there to help you get started.

We Believe that through the Atonement of Christ, all mankind may Be saved, By obedience to the laws and ordinances of the Gospel.

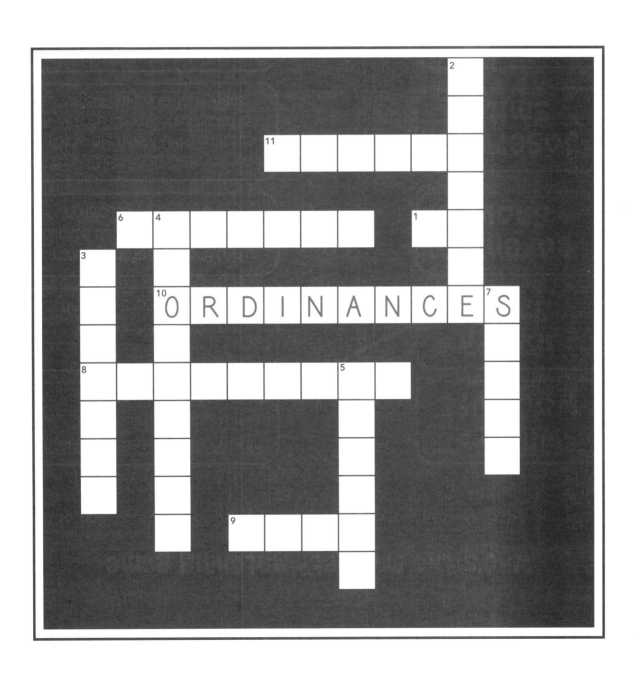

Do you Believe that the Church President is a Prophet of God?

What Does this mean to you?

God wants to help His people. He wants to keep them safe. He wants them to know how to choose the right. One of the ways Heavenly Father helps us is by giving us a prophet to lead us.

A prophet will teach us about Heavenly Father and Jesus Christ. He will bear a special testimony and witness of Heavenly Father and His gospel.

Prophets will also help us know the things that Heavenly Father wants us to be doing. They will teach us the truth. Prophets speak the truth even when others in the world may not like what they are saying. We will find safety and peace when we choose to listen to and obey what the Prophet tells us to do.

Directions: Draw a face on the President of the Church below so he looks like our Church President. Then fill in the speech bubbles around him with things he tells us to do.

SCRIPTURES

2 Chronicles 20:20, Amos 3:7, 1 Nephi 22:1–2,
Doctrine and Covenants 107:91–92, Articles of Faith 1:6

Sixth Article of Faith

Directions: Using the words provided, see if you can fill in the blanks in the sixth article of faith below.

We _____ in the same _____ that existed in the _____ Church, namely, apostles,_____, pastors, teachers,_____, and so _____.

organization, evangelists, Primitive, forth, believe, prophets

What a Great Prophet We Have!

Directions: Fill in the blanks below about our current prophet.

The man who was prophet when I was born was _____

Our current prophet is _____

The date he became prophet was _____

His wife's name is _____

He has _____ children

He grew up in _____

Some interesting facts about him that I learned _____

_____

I asked an adult who the prophet was when they got baptized, and it was _____

Some things they remember about him are _____

_____

97

Who's the Prophet? Matching game

Directions: Match the name of the prophet on the left to the description of the prophet on the right. The first one is done for you.

Wilford Woodruff	First President of the Church Restored the gospel of Jesus Christ.
Joseph Smith	Second President of the Church Led the pioneers to Utah.
Lorenzo Snow	Third President of the Church Organized the church-wide adoption of the Primary Association.
Joseph F. Smith	Fourth President of the Church Issued the 1890 Manifesto which officially ended the Church's support of plural marriage.
Brigham Young	Fifth President of the Church The Church adopted the principle of tithing as a key part of being a member.
Heber J. Grant	Sixth President of the Church First Church president to travel outside of North America as a prophet.
George Albert Smith	Seventh President of the Church Founded the Church's welfare program.
John Taylor	Eighth President of the Church World War II ended while he was president.

Harold B. Lee	Ninth President of the Church Began plans for what eventually became BYU–Hawaii.
Ezra Taft Benson	Tenth President of the Church Dedicated the Ogden and Provo Utah Temples.
Thomas S. Monson	Eleventh President of the Church The BYU–Provo Library is named after him.
David O. McKay	Twelfth President of the Church First Missionary Training Center was dedicated under him.
Gordon B. Hinckley	Thirteenth President of the Church Emphasized reading The Book of Mormon.
Russell M. Nelson	Fourteenth President of the Church Every member should have a temple recommend.
Joseph Fielding Smith	Fifteenth President of the Church Known for accelerating the building of temples. When he became president, there were 47 operating temples in the church. When he died, there were 124.
Howard W. Hunter	Sixteenth President of the Church Served in several adult Scouting leadership capacities and received the Silver Beaver in Scouting.
Spencer W. Kimball	Seventeenth President of the Church All worthy baptized members can serve as a witness at a baptism.

Follow the Path of the Prophets

Directions: Below are several different paths you can take. One path follows the things that the prophets have asked us to do. Follow the path that provides direction from the prophets to find joy.

Question: Which path will you follow?

Answer: _____

3

Read the Book of Mormon   Attend Seminary

2

Don't set goals   Sleep During general conference

4

Watch cartoons all Day   Only read comic Books

Set goals

1

Stretch the truth

Eat all the snacks you want

5

Be unkind to others

Skip seminary With friends

Eat healthy

Watch general conference

Taking the sacrament each week

helps us remember our baptismal covenants and stay on the covenant path

You have learned many wonderful things about your baptism and the covenants you will make. You can be excited and happy to be taking this step in your life. Choosing to be baptized puts you on the covenant path with Heavenly Father. Being on this path will help you continue to make wise choices and be close to God.

President Nelson said, "We choose to live and progress on the Lord's covenant path and to stay on it. It is not a complicated way. It is the way to true joy in this life and eternal life beyond" (Russell M. Nelson, Christmas Devotional, December 2, 2018).

Don't worry if you do not feel like you have everything figured out just yet. You will keep growing as you continue to go to church, read the scriptures, and study with your family.

Heavenly Father has also given you the sacrament so that every week you can remember the promises you made when you were baptized. Each week when you attend sacrament meeting, you are able to take the bread and water. Jesus taught us in the Bible that the bread and water help us remember that Jesus lived and died for us. Taking the sacrament allows us to renew the covenants we made at baptism.

SCRIPTURES

Moroni 4:3, Moroni 5:2, Luke 22:19–20

Covenant Path Crossword Puzzle

Directions: Solve the crossword puzzle by putting the correct word for each activity in the right place.

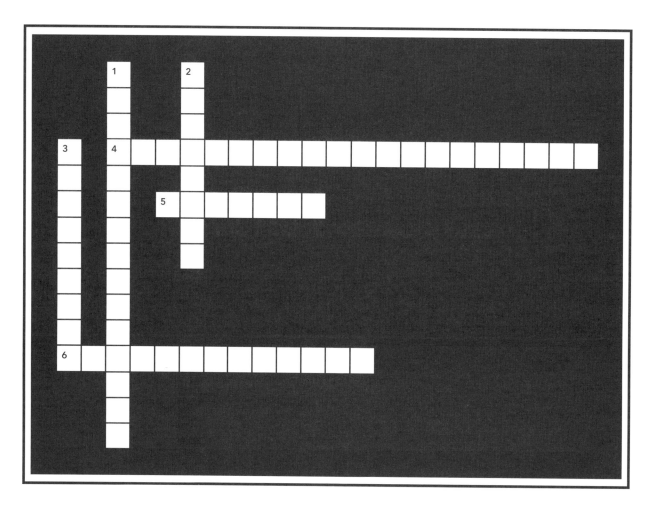

Down

1. A religious ceremony administered in temples of The Church of Jesus Christ of Latter-day Saints.

2. A promise made between God and a person or a group of people.

3. The ordinance in which participants eat bread and drink water in remembrance of the body and blood of Jesus Christ.

Across

4. The power and authority of God given to man, including the authority to perform ordinances and to act as a leader in the Church.

5. Immersion in water is necessary for an individual to become a member of The Church of Jesus Christ of Latter-day Saints.

6. An ordinance performed in the temple that eternally unites a husband and wife or children and their parents.

When I take the sacrament, I renew my Baptismal Covenants

Directions: On the pieces of bread below, you can see the promises that you make and the promises that God makes when you take the sacrament and renew your baptismal covenants. Color each piece of bread, and on the lines provided, write whether it's a promise you make or a promise God makes.

KEEP HIS COMMANDMENTS

ALWAYS HAVE HIS SPIRIT TO BE WITH US

ALWAYS REMEMBER HIM

TAKE ON THE NAME OF HIS SON (JESUS)

Answer Key

Page 4 crossword puzzle

Down:
1. Burdens
3. Mourning
5. Those
6. Bearing
8. Need

Across:
2. Called
4. Comforting
7. God
9. People
10. Witness

Page 11 ordinances

Baptism: Bear one another burdens.
Baptism: Mourn with those that mourn.
Baptism: Comfort those that stand in need.
Baptism: Stand as a witness of God.
Sacrament: Always remember Him.
Sacrament: Keep His commandments.
Sacrament: That you may always have His spirit.

Page 29 Twelfth Article of Faith

We believe in being subject to kings, presidents, rulers, and magistrates, in obeying, honoring, and sustaining the law.

Page 31 Thirteenth Article of Faith

We believe in being honest, true, chaste, benevolent, virtuous, and in doing good to all men; indeed, we may say that we follow the admonition of Paul-We believe all things, we hope all things, we have endured many things, and hope to be able to endure all things. If there is anything virtuous, lovely, or of good report or praiseworthy, we seek after these things.

Page 5 maze

Page 30 wordsearch

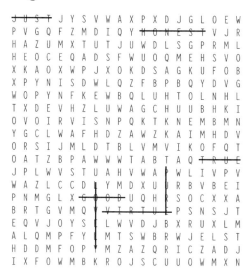

Page 8 wordsearch

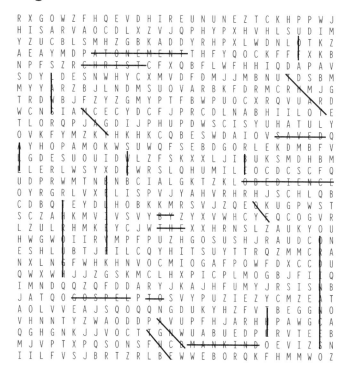

Page 46 wordsearch

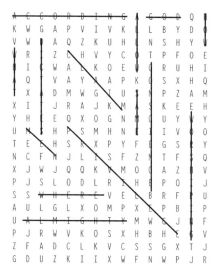

Answer Key

Page 36 maze

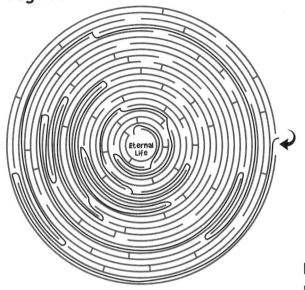

Eternal Life

Page 66 wordsearch

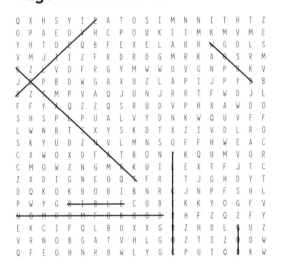

Page 95 crossword puzzle

Down:
2. Believe
3. Through
4. Atonement
5. Christ
7. Saved

Across:
1. We
6. Mankind
8. Obedience
9. Laws
10. Ordinances
11. Gospel

Page 102 crossword puzzle

Down:
1. Temple Endowment
2. Covenant
3. Sacrament

Across:
4. Priesthood Ordination
5. Baptism
6. Temple Sealing

Page 62 Seventh Article of Faith

We believe in the gift of tongues, prophecy, revelation, visions, healing, interpretation of tongues, and and so forth.

Page 74 First Article of Faith

We believe in God, the Eternal Father, and in His Son, Jesus Christ, and in the Holy Ghost.

Page 97 The Sixth Article of Faith

We believe in the same organization that existed in the Primitive Church, namely, apostles, prophets, pastors, teachers, evangelists, and so forth.

Page 77 The Holy Ghost Comforts

Doctrine and Covenants 121:46: The Holy Ghost shall be thy constant a companion, and thy scepter an unchanging scepter of righteousness and truth; and thy dominion shall be an everlasting dominion, and without compulsory means it shall flow unto thee forever and ever.

2 Nephi 31:12: And also, the voice of the Son came unto me, saying: He that is baptized in my name, to him will the Father give the Holy Ghost, like unto me; wherefore, follow me, and do the things which ye have seen me do.

Page 98–99 matching game

Joseph Smith: First President of the Church.

Brigham Young: Second President of the Church.

John Taylor: Third President of the Church.

Wilford Woodruff: Fourth President of the Church.

Lorenzo Snow: Fifth President of the Church.

Joseph F. Smith: Sixth President of the Church.

Heber J. Grant: Seventh President of the Church.

George Albert Smith: Eighth President of the Church.

David O. McKay: Ninth President of the Church

Joseph Fielding Smith: Tenth President of the Church.

Harold B. Lee: Eleventh President of the Church

Spencer W. Kimball: Twelfth President of the Church.

Ezra Taft Benson: Thirteenth President of the Church.

Howard W. Hunter: Fourteenth President of the Church.

Gordon B. Hinckley: Fifteenth President of the Church.

Thomas S. Monson: Sixteenth President of the Church.

Russell M. Nelson: Seventeenth President of the Church.

ABout the Author

KATIE EDNA STEED wears many hats and carries various titles. Currently she serves as the disability specialist manager for The Church of Jesus Christ of Latter-day Saints. Prior to this, she spent fifteen years as an associate clinical professor at Brigham Young University in the Department of Counseling Psychology and Special Education. Her area of expertise is teaching children with severe disabilities, including autism. She taught the methods and practicum courses for fifteen years at Brigham Young University for students who would like to become licensed special educators. Before teaching at Brigham Young University, Katie taught in public schools both as a general educator and a special educator.

Her thesis is entitled, "Instructing Teachers of Children with Disabilities within The Church of Jesus Christ of Latter-day Saints." She is passionate about this topic and has presented at BYU's Education Week and several churches of various faiths over the past twenty years on how to best instruct individuals with differing abilities.

Katie also serves alongside her husband as a technical specialist for Latter-day Saint Charities, where she provides training throughout the world to help educators, medical personnel, and parents know how to support individuals with autism and other such conditions.

Katie's favorite titles are that of wife and mother to her husband and her three wonderful children, one of which has autism. She loves to support children of all abilities and their parents as they work to achieve their goals and become what they desire to be.

KatieEDnasteeD.com